TIME SPACE AND DRUMS PART 1....

ROCK
DRUMMING
Development

TIME SPACE AND DRUMS PART THREE

ROCK
DRUMMING
Development

CONSTELLATIONS Volume 1

The Time Space & Drums Series
A Complete Program of Lessons in Professional, Contemporary Rock and Jazz
Drumming Styles.

Written and Developed By:
Stephen Hawkins

Graphic Design By: Nathaniel Dasco.
Special Thanks To Linda Drouin and Ikhide Oshoma

ThinkeLife Publications

Stephen Hawkins - Time Space and Drums
Visit my website at www.timespaceanddrums.com

First printing: August 2020.

ISBN: 978 1 913929 02 2

Dedicated to the late Paul Daniels and family, Martin Daniels, Trevor Daniels, Paul Mellor's, Keith, Peter Windle, Andrew Marple's, Colin Keys, Peters & Lee, Susan Maughan, Ronnie Dukes, Tom O'Connor, Les Dennis, Bob Monkhouse, Bobby Davro, Tommy Bruce, Robert Young, Sandie Gold as well as the hundreds of other people who have played a part in my life experience. Including Sphinx Entertainment, E & B Productions as well as the hundreds of fantastic personalities I have had the pleasure of working alongside over the past 35 years. Apologies for anyone I have missed, not forgetting the current reader who I hope will receive as much from their drumming as I have and more – Stephen Hawkins.

Table of Contents

DRUM ROLL, PLEASE! Getting Started 1

Lesson 1: Bass Drum Development Exercises 3

Lesson 2: Snare Drum Development Exercises 9

Lesson 3: Bass Drum and Snare Drum Combination Development Exercises.............. 15

Lesson 4: 1/16th Note Variations on the Bass Drum 21

Lesson 5: Mixed Variations Using 1/16th Notes 1 30

Lesson 6: Mixed Variations Using 1/16th Notes 2 43

RUDIMENTARY 52

Double Stroke Roll 52

The Double Stroke 52

The Double Stroke Roll 53

CONSTELLATIONS Volume 1 54

Featured Drummer Recommendations 55

Conclusion 56

DRUM ROLL, PLEASE! Getting Started

Congratulations! Give yourself a pat on the back for getting this far in the series.

You should by now have completed books 1 and 2 and should have a solid rock and jazz foundation of drumming skills. If you are already an intermediate drummer then these exercises will help you get a tighter grip of reading music as well as playing in general.

It's now time to develop and start building on that foundation. However, you should make absolutely sure that you have a firm grip of that foundation first, covered in books 1 and 2 of the series. If not please review books 1 and 2 to make absolutely sure that you are comfortable with all of those foundational skills. This is essential for the successful conclusion of this part of the series and the following book 4.

If on the other hand, you are confident of your solid foundation skills, and that it is comfortably mastered, then and only then should you proceed with this part of the program.

Obviously, you have now taken this third step and proven yourself to be determined to succeed. But before we continue please understand that a vital part of the Time Space and Drums Series is to download the free audio demonstration files for each part, not just for the demonstrations themselves, but because I have included additional tips and guidance in what I call the Essence emails. You receive a written email version and an audio version so you can better grasp those concepts. That said, let us continue.

This book takes all of the exercises from book 1 (Rock Foundation) and builds on them by varying the snare drum pattern and the bass drum patterns. And then to combine the bass and snare drum patterns with some variations.

All of the exercises are demonstrated for you in the free audio download files available by registering at timespaceanddrums.com, so you can listen to each lesson to see what the various rhythms sound like as well as learning to read the exercise on paper from a purely theoretical point of view.

Study the exercise mathematically from this book to assure a basic understanding, then listen to the exercise as demonstrated to see how it sounds. Then when you have the exercise firmly in mind, attempt to play the exercise.

If you have any difficulty, play one limb at a time in order to get the basic rhythm and motion of each limb within the exercise you are practicing, and how the parts fit together physically. Then attempt to put it all together.

All of the exercises are demonstrated with the right hand on the HH. It is then up to you to rework them by adding the left foot on the HH, beats 1, 2, 3 and 4. And then play the RH on the ride cymbal as we covered in books 1 and 2.

This will all take added time and it would also be a good idea to rewrite the exercises in a manuscript pad with the RH on the Ride Cymbal and the 4 beats of the HH on beats 1, 2, 3 and 4. Then try playing the LF HH on beats 2 and 4 only.

By writing the exercises you will gain a better understanding of the exercise itself as well as rhythmic music in general. Don't cut corners and you will make it. What else is there to do anyway? Good Luck and Have Fun!

Stephen Hawkins.

Free Audio Demonstrations

You should first visit the following URL to download audio demonstrations of every exercise in this book as soon as possible. You will then receive additional tips and guidance through the included essence emails.

www.timespaceanddrums.com/tsd-3rt.html

Before continuing with the first lesson, you should skip to page 52 and read the Rudimentary section as we have done in the previous books in the series. Although in this instance it isn't absolutely necessary, we do recommend you to begin learning the rudimentary information covered on page 52. You can then return here and begin lesson 1 starting on the next page.

Lesson 1

Bass Drum Development Exercises

We begin the first lesson by developing the bass drum using the 1/8th note rock beat. As always, the exercises should be played slowly, to begin with then gradually speed the tempo until you can play it at various tempos. However, don't try to play them to fast to soon. Strive for a high degree of precision, and to make the exercises flow.

Exercise 1

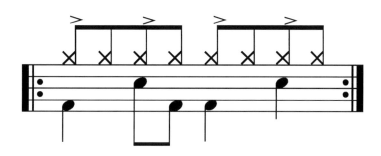

Exercise 2

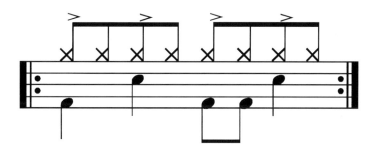

Exercise 3

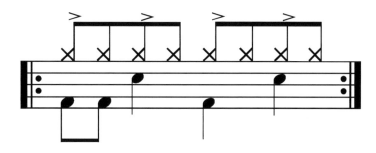

Exercise 4

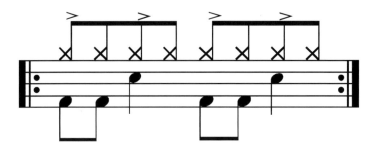

Exercise 5

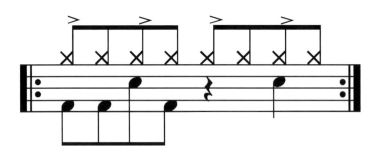

Exercise 6

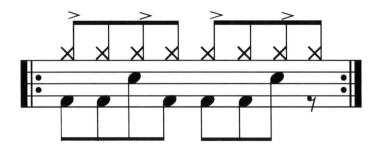

Exercise 7

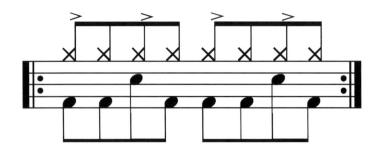

Exercise 8

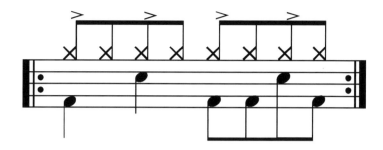

Exercise 9

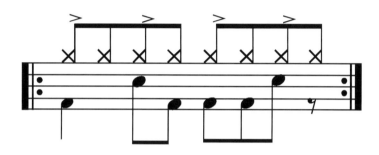

Exercise 10

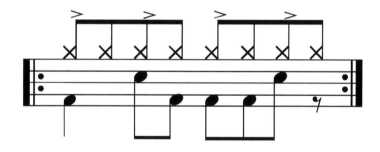

Exercise 11

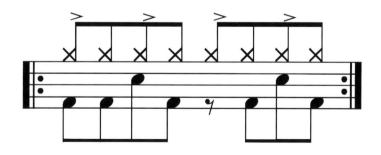

Exercise 12

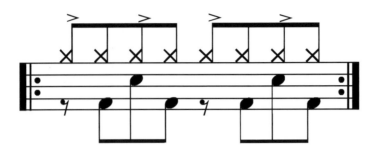

Exercise 13

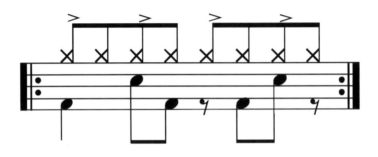

Exercise 14

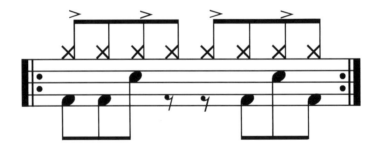

Exercise 15

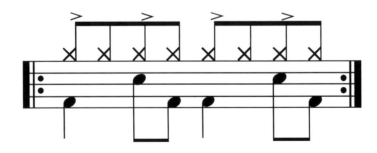

Exercise 16

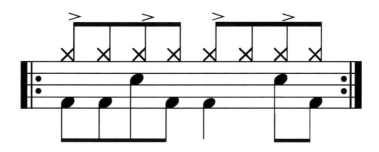

Exercise 17

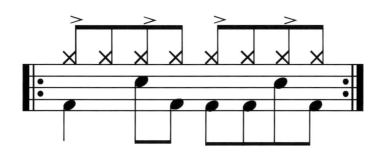

Exercise 18

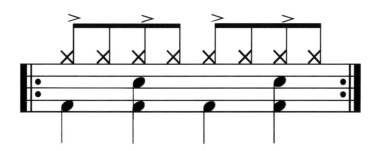

Exercise 19

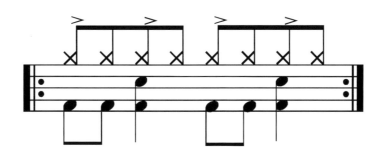

Exercise 20

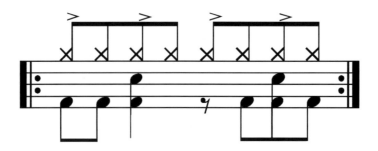

Exercise 21

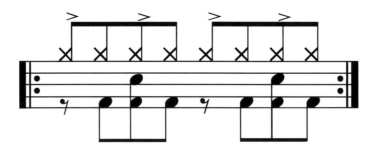

Exercise 22

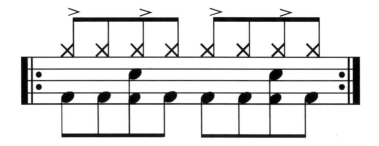

Lesson 2

Snare Drum Development Exercises

Now we'll move on to developing the snare drum with a 1/8th note rock beat. Again, start slowly, and then repeat the lesson at a slightly faster tempo, then again, a little faster.

Exercise 1

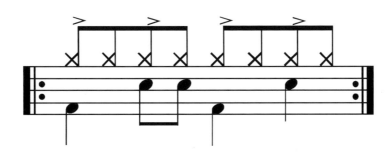

Exercise 2

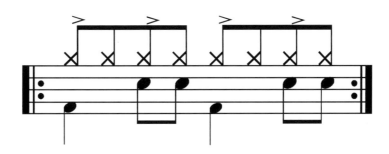

Exercise 3

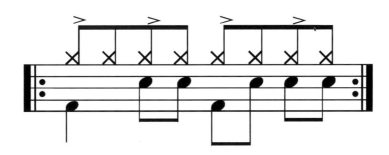

Exercise 4

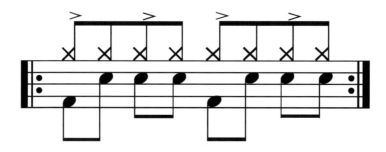

Exercise 5

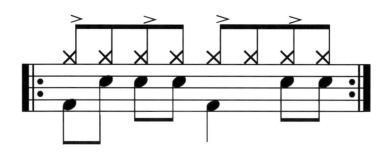

Exercise 6

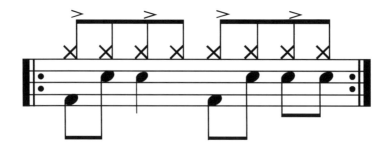

Exercise 7

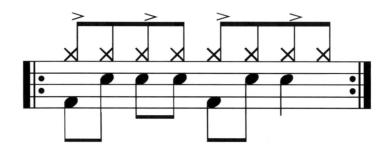

Exercise 8

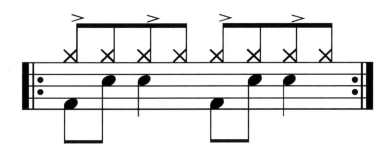

Exercise 9

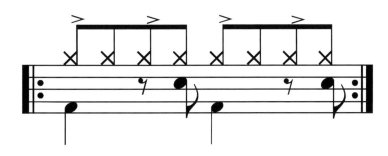

Exercise 10

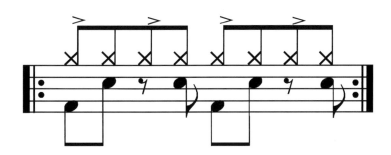

Exercise 11

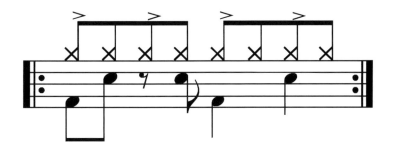

Exercise 12

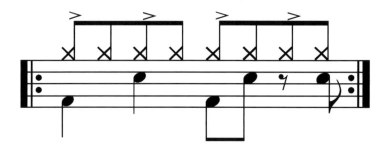

Exercise 13

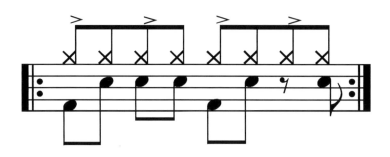

Exercise 14

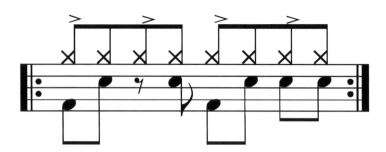

Exercise 15

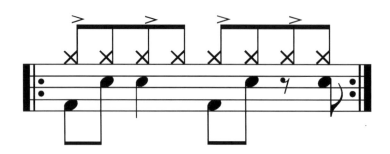

Exercise 16

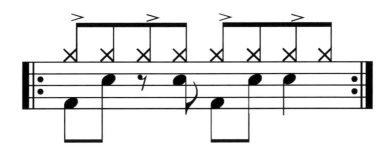

Exercise 17

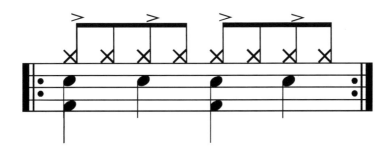

Exercise 18

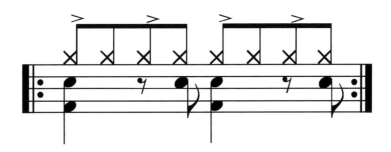

Exercise 19

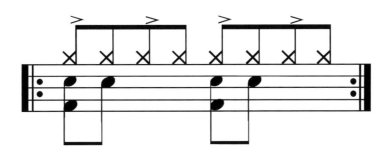

Exercise 20

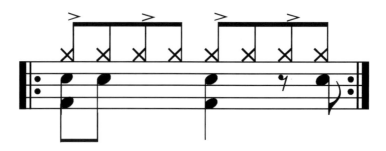

Exercise 21

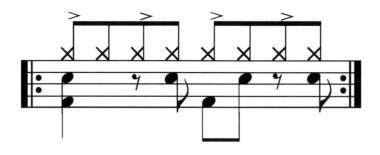

Exercise 22

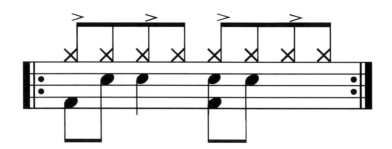

Lesson 3

Bass Drum and Snare Drum Combination Development Exercises

The next step is to mix the bass drum and snare drum with a 1/8th note rock beat. Again, start slowly and repeat at a faster tempo

Exercise 1

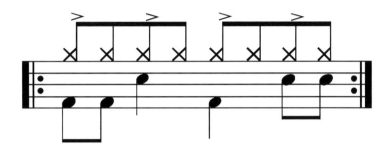

Exercise 2

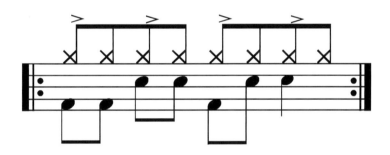

Exercise 3

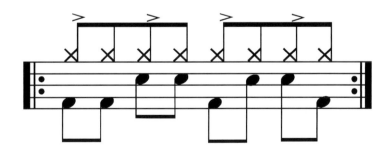

Exercise 4

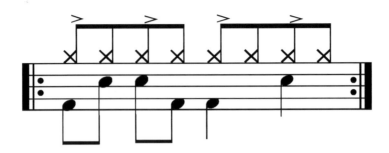

Exercise 5

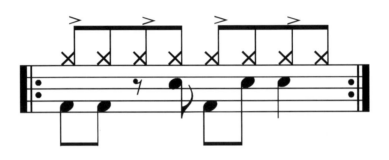

Exercise 6

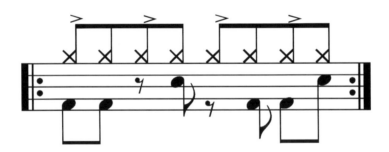

Exercise 7

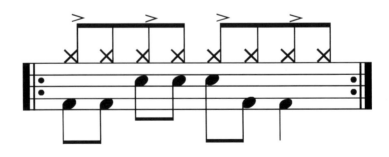

Exercise 8

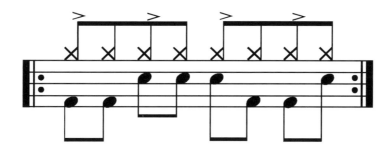

Exercise 9

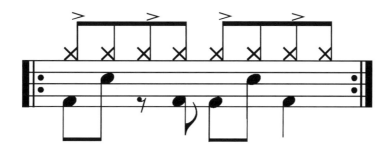

Exercise 10

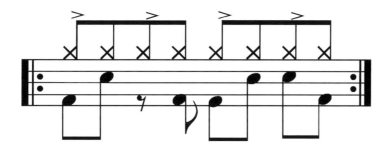

Exercise 11

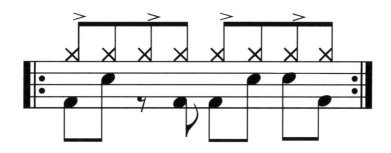

Exercise 12

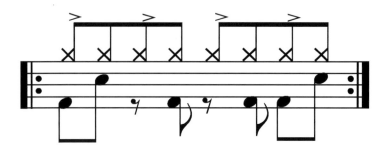

Exercise 13

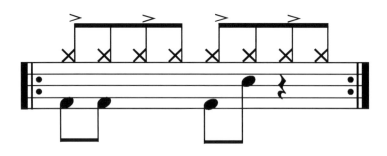

Exercise 14

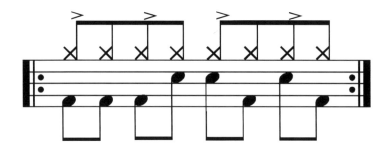

Exercise 15

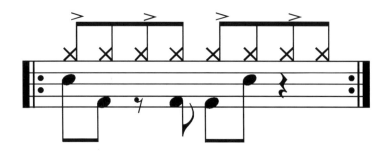

Exercise 16

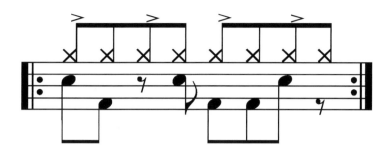

Exercise 17

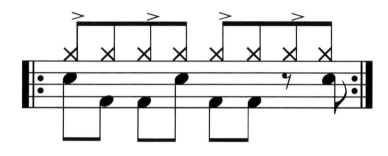

Exercise 18

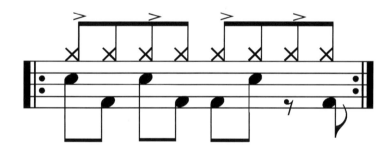

Exercise 19

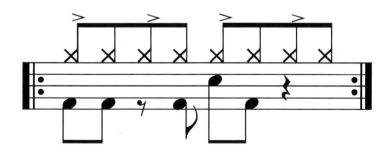

Exercise 20

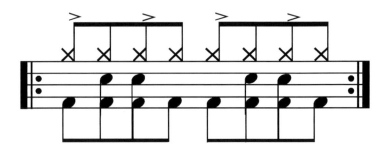

Exercise 21

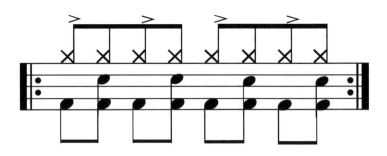

Exercise 22

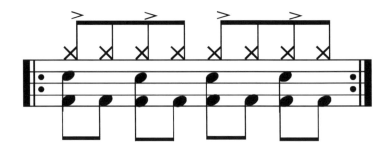

Lesson 4

1/16th Note Variations on the Bass Drum

In this lesson, we will add 1/16th notes in order to spice the beats up a little. First, practice these samba style rhythms on the bass drum and snare drum, against the 1/8th note rock beat HH pattern. This rhythm is easier if you think of it as the notes on the beat being slightly louder than the 1/16th notes in-between the 1/8th notes. The two beats sort of snap together.

Exercise 1a

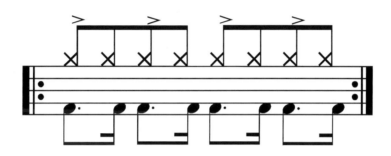

Exercise 1b

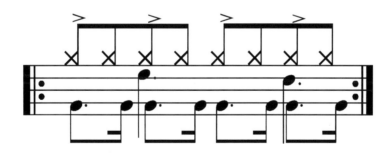

Exercise 1c

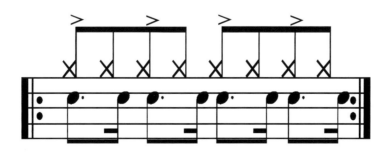

Exercise 1d

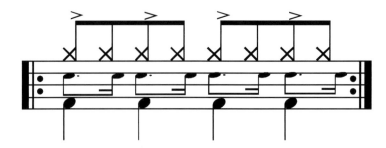

Now let's develop the 1/16th notes on the snare drum

Exercise 1

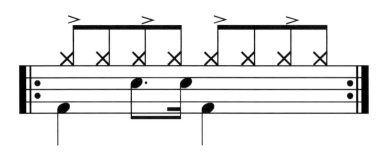

Exercise 2

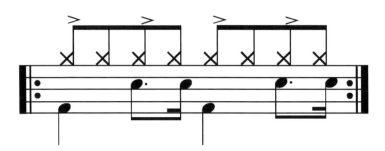

Exercise 3

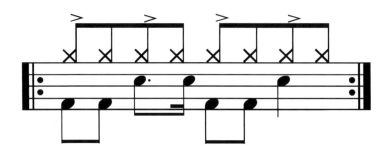

Exercise 4

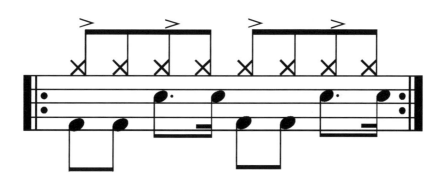

Exercise 5

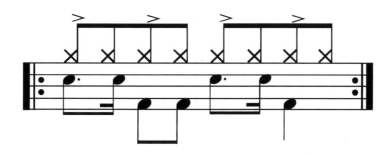

Exercise 6

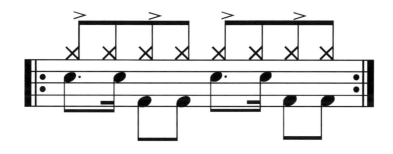

Exercise 7

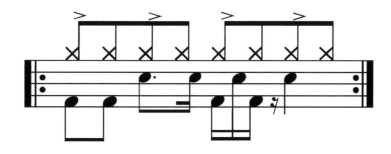

Exercise 8

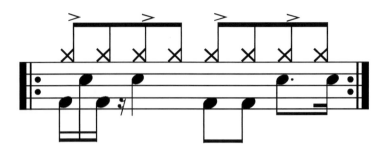

Exercise 9

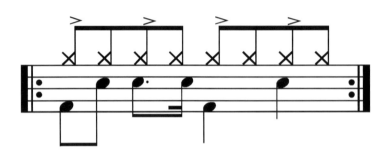

Exercise 10

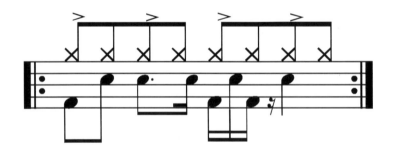

Exercise 11

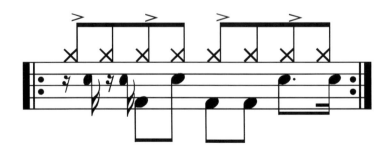

This time we will develop the 1/16th notes on the bass drum

Exercise 1

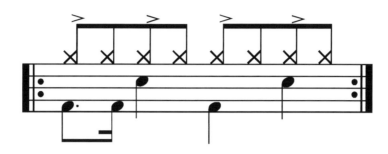

Exercise 2

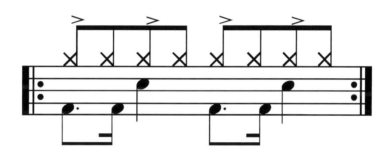

Exercise 3

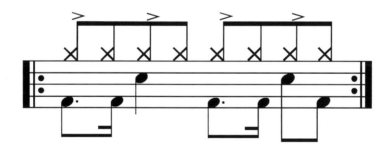

Exercise 4

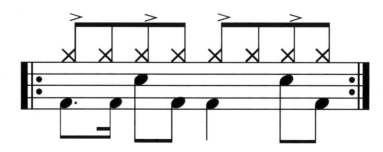

Exercise 5

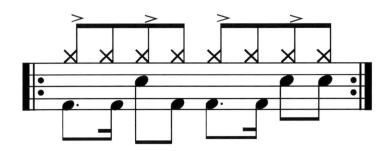

Exercise 6

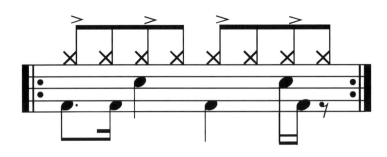

Exercise 7

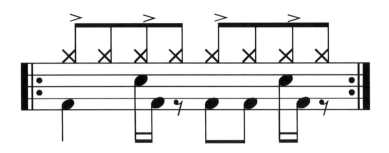

Exercise 8

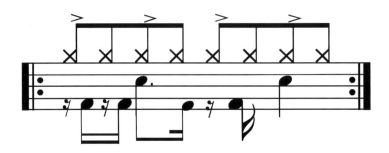

Exercise 9

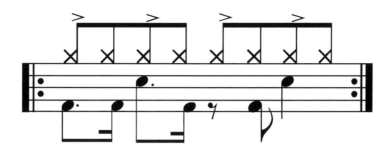

Exercise 10

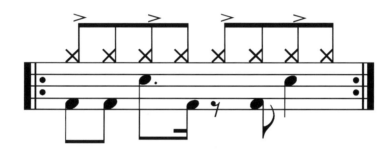

Exercise 11

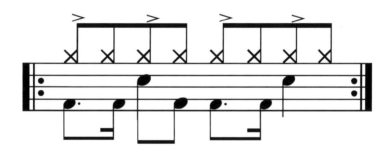

Exercise 12

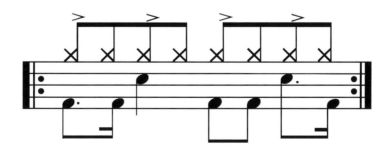

Now let's try a few mixed SD BD 1/16th note exercises.

Exercise 1

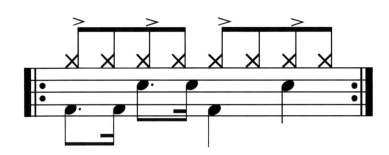

Exercise 2

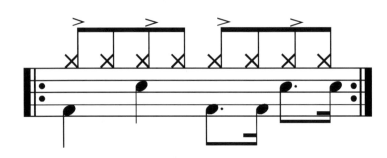

Exercise 3

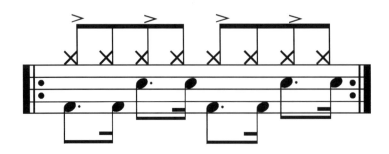

Exercise 4

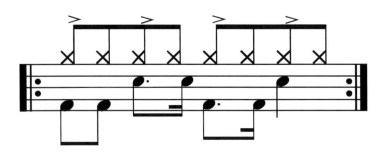

Exercise 5

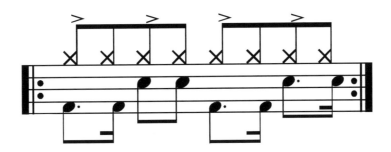

Exercise 6

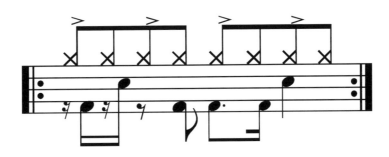

Exercise 7

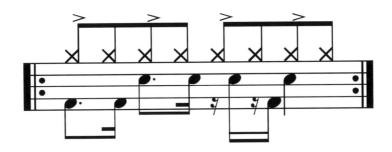

Lesson 5

Mixed Variations Using 1/16th Notes 1.

Now let's take a look at some 1/4, 1/8th, and 1/16th note variation bass drum and snare drum exercises. You should listen to the Audio Demonstration and become familiar with the sound of each exercise before attempting to play them. Let's begin with some 1/4 note rock beat exercises.

Exercise 1

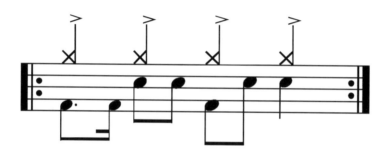

Exercise 2

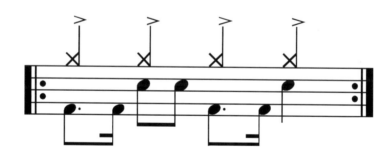

Exercise 3

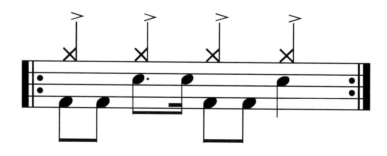

Exercise 4

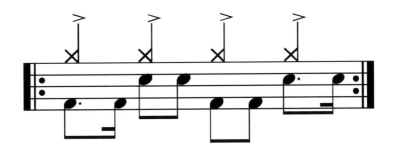

Exercise 5

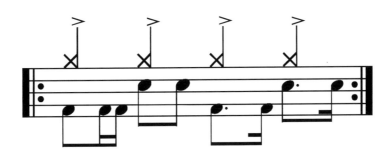

Exercise 6

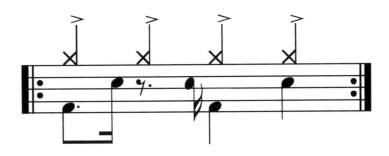

Exercise 7

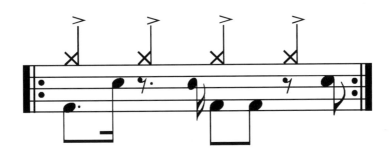

Exercise 8

Exercise 9

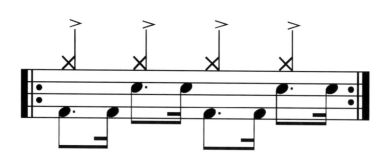

Exercise 10

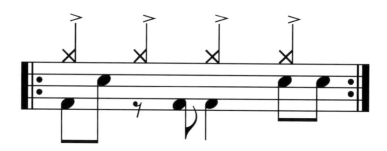

Exercise 11

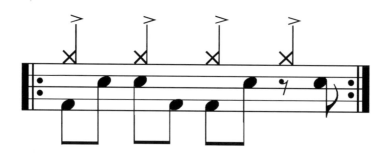

Exercise 12

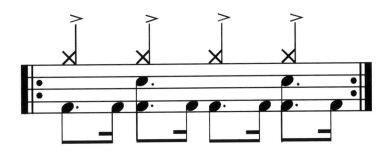

Now let's try some 1/16th note rhythm exercises.

Exercise 1

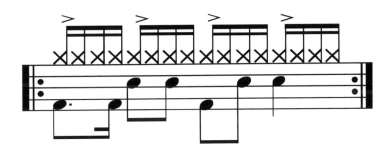

Exercise 2

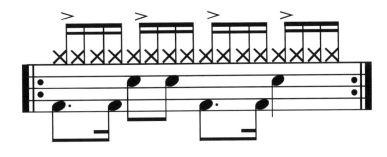

Exercise 3

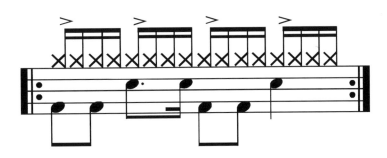

Exercise 4

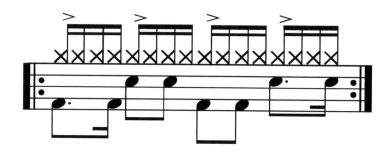

Exercise 5

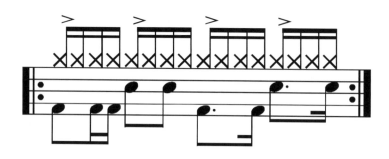

Exercise 6

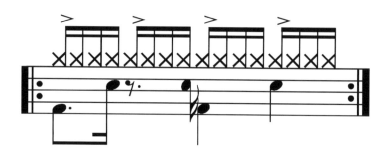

Exercise 7

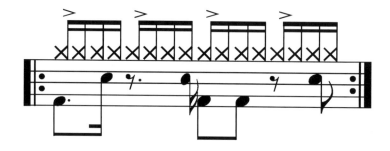

Exercise 8

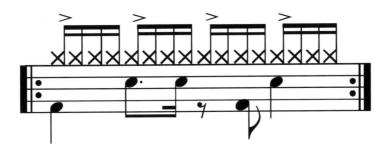

Exercise 9

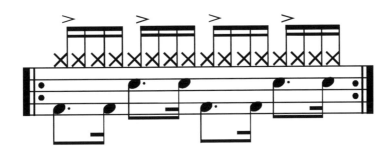

Exercise 10

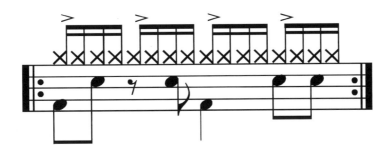

Exercise 11

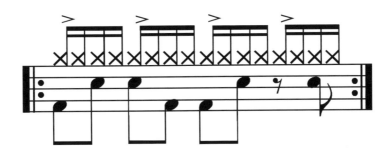

Exercise 12

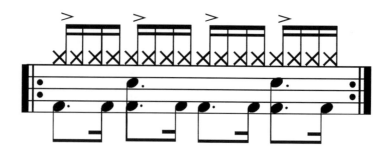

This time we'll try some 1/16th note variation exercises

Exercise 1

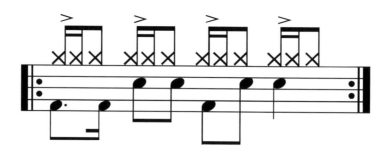

Exercise 2

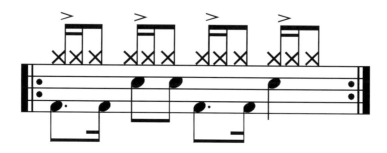

Exercise 3

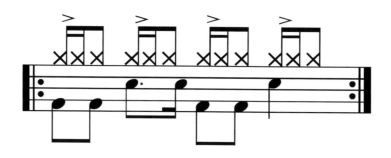

Exercise 4

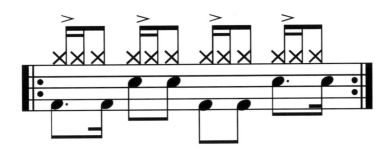

Exercise 5

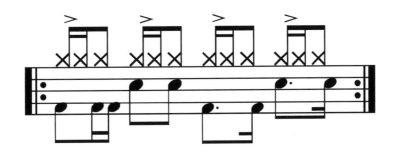

Exercise 6

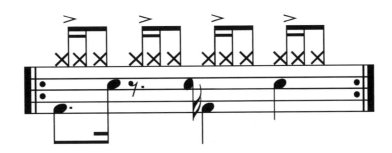

Exercise 7

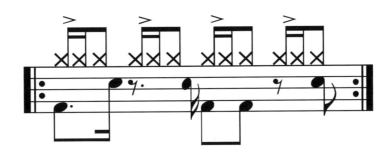

Exercise 8

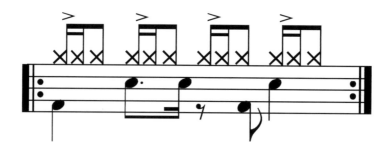

Exercise 9

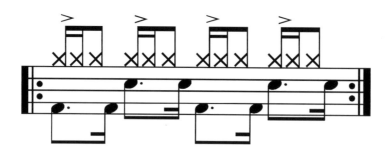

Exercise 10

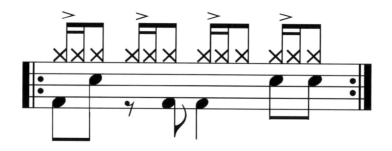

Exercise 11

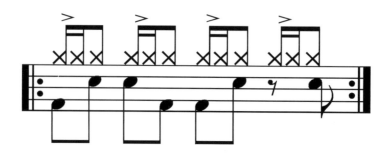

Exercise 12

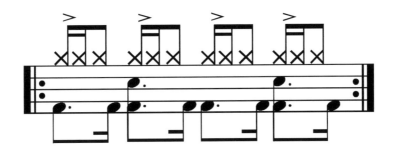

This time we'll play some 1/16th note variation 2 exercises

Exercise 1

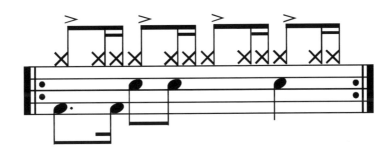

Exercise 2

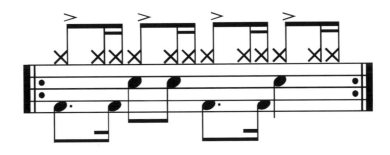

Exercise 3

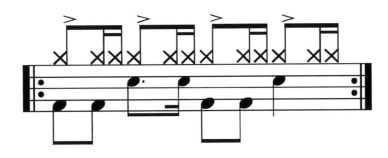

Exercise 4

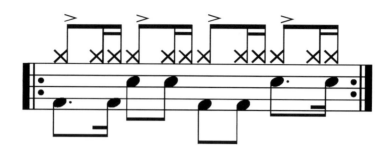

Exercise 5

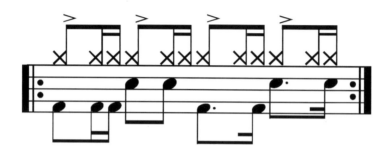

Exercise 6

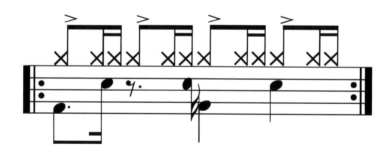

Exercise 7

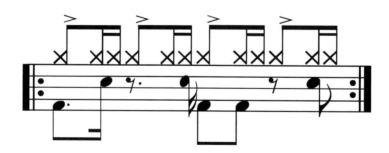

Exercise 8

Exercise 9

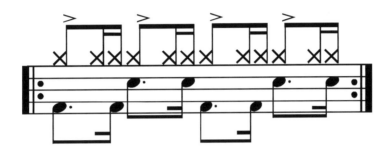

Exercise 10

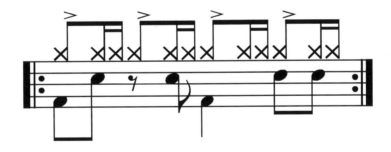

Exercise 11

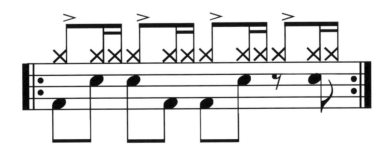

Exercise 12

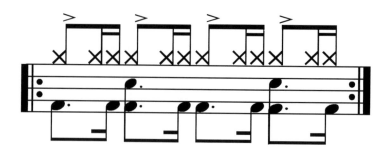

Lesson 6

Mixed Variations Using 1/16th Notes 2

We will complete the final part of this book by applying all of the rock style rhythms that we have covered and mix the bass and snare drum patterns. When you have completed all of these exercises you should begin again playing the RH on the ride cymbal and beats 1, 2, 3 and 4 on the LF HH.

The first set of exercises is the disco style HH pattern with the RH HH. Again, you should repeat them with the RH ride cymbal and beats 1, 2, 3 and 4 played on the LF HH.

Exercise 1

Exercise 2

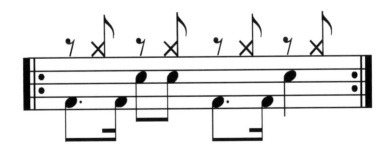

Exercise 3

Exercise 4

Exercise 5

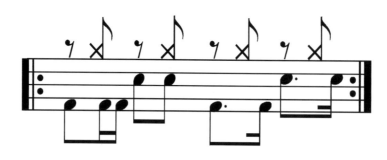

Exercise 6

Exercise 7

Exercise 8

Exercise 9

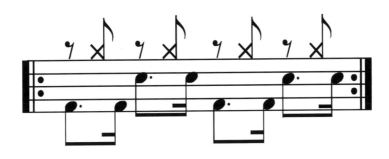

Exercise 10

Exercise 11

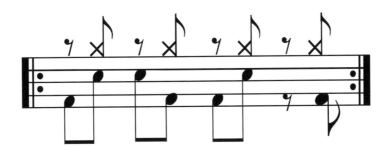

Exercise 12

1/8th note exercises

Exercise 1

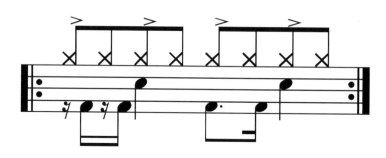

Exercise 2

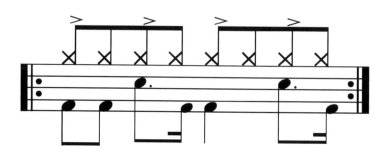

Exercise 3

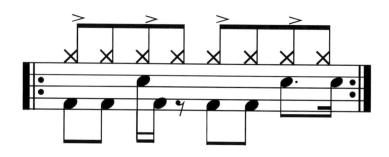

Exercise 4

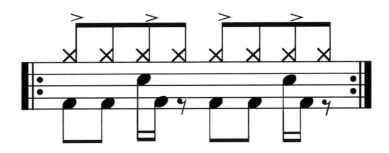

Exercise 5

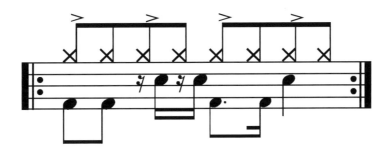

1/16th note exercises.

Exercise 1

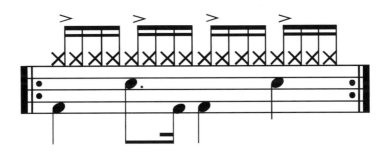

Exercise 2

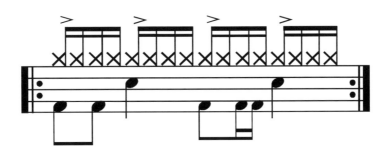

Exercise 3

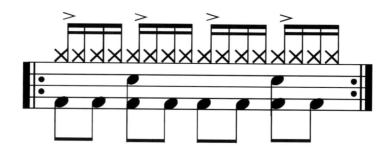

1/4 note exercises.

Exercise 1

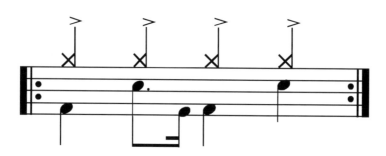

Exercise 2

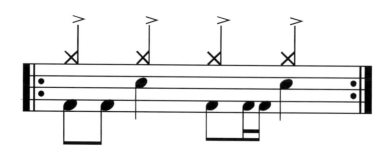

Exercise 3

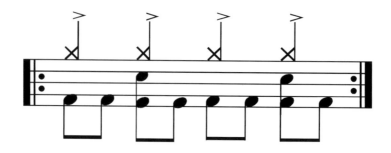

1/16th note variations 1.

Exercise 1

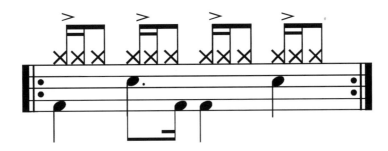

Exercise 2

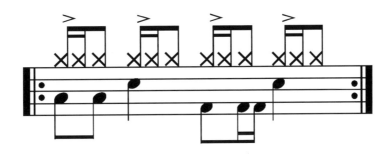

Exercise 3

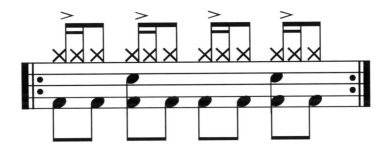

1/16th note variations 2

Exercise 1

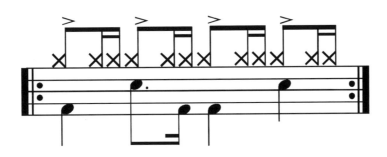

Exercise 2

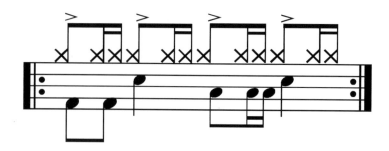

Exercise 3

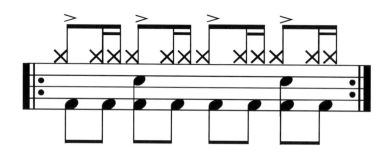

Disco style beat exercises

Exercise 1

Exercise 2

Exercise 3

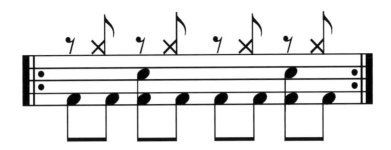

RUDIMENTARY

Double Stroke Roll

If you remember in the first Rudimentary section in book 1, I mentioned that I wasn't much of a rudimentary drummer. Well, this is where that statement changes slightly simply because we are discussing a subject that I am much more comfortable with. The double stroke roll.

It seems to me that if you are going to play something that required the speed or number of notes necessary to be called a roll, then why play single strokes at all. If I was going to play 2, 4, 8 or more strokes on any particular drum then why would I need single strokes at all?

Of course, there are scenarios where single strokes help such as playing a single stroke on one drum with one hand followed by another single stroke on another drum but it also occurs to me that that is a rare occurrence as far as I can tell. That isn't to say that you should skip over single stroke rolls as they are an important part of the whole development process and become more important when you begin to do combination exercises, but we aren't there yet so let's get back on point.

You should absolutely put everything into practicing your single stroke rolls simply because the above statements are as close as you can get to a rationalization on my own past stemming from the fact that double strokes just seem more logical.

That doesn't mean to say I didn't spend hours per day for months in my early years playing nine stroke rolls (for example) leading with the left hand for the first nine strokes and then leading with the right hand for the second nine strokes and so on because I did. The difference for me was that I never really did the same with single stroke rolls until later in life and believe me the earlier you get this practice done the better for you over the long term. Please also take into mind that I am pretty hard on myself when it comes to my abilities in any area and so it will never be good enough for me.

The Double Stroke

So now we have that out of the way let's get down to the second rudiment and again, it should be noted that this whole book is centered around the double stoke rudiment but in a lesser degree than the single stroke was the underlying theme of the first book.

As one of the most basic fundamentals of drumming you will be using it throughout your drumming career so like the single stroke roll the double stroke roll needs to be practiced over many weeks, months and years in order to improve and eventually perfect it.

This rudiment is really just hitting the drum once as before and then controlling the bounce of that first stroke to hit the drum again and then snapping your fingers around the drum stick to gain control of the stick and then repeating this movement. That's it in a nutshell.

We call this a stroke, or a double stroke. This double stroke hand movement should be practiced individually with each of the two hands before attempting to put the two hands together but that is the next step.

After practicing the basic arm and hand movements as described above it is time to turn the double strokes into a double stroke roll.

The Double Stroke Roll

The double stroke roll is exactly as it sounds. Do a double stroke with the right-hand and then do a double stroke with the left-hand all on the same drum or practice pad.

You then simply repeat those two strokes so the pattern begins to look like this:

R R, L L, R R, L L.

There is no need to practice this at speed as the actual movements need to be practiced first. As you can see, I made the first of each double stroke on each hand larger so you can better see what the stroke should sound like. right, right, left, left and so on. If you refer back to the notation diagram in book 1 on page 16 you can see that the above exercise includes 8 strokes or notes just like the single stroke roll did and so you can see that the double stroke exercise above is a 1/8th note exercise. i.e. 8 x 1/8th notes in a single bar of 4/4 music.

When you are comfortable playing the double strokes using 1/8th notes you can try doubling up by using twice as many notes (16) just as we did before in book 1. The exercise then becomes a 1/16th note exercise.

R R L L, R R L L, R R L L, R R L L.

And again, as before both of the examples above are played at the same speed but one has 8 notes in a bar and the other has 16 notes in a bar.

You can double up again and have 32 x 1/32nd notes in the bar but that is beyond the scope of this initial set of lessons. However, the goal is to eventually play single as well as double stroke rolls using 32nd notes but as suggested do not rush this as it is more important to get the technique right than it is to play the rudiments faster.

If you need to, you should read this section again and then practice the double strokes followed by the double stroke roll until you can play it smoothly and evenly. Then return to the beginning of the book and carry on with the first lesson. But as before, take your time as you don't need to get it perfect before moving on, just begin practicing the movements.

CONSTELLATIONS Volume 1

So, what does that mean? Why constellations and what does a constellation have to do with drumming? Constellations are from our point of view, groups of drum beats.

The term constellation is used to describe an imaginary outline of stars that are grouped together within space, the constellation is usually given the name of an animal, or other creature as well as mythological people and even inanimate objects.

Much like in musical terms the constellations were used to describe beliefs or attitudes held by people or groups of people and so a group of notes or varying notes could be described as a constellation of notes, but in our case we are speaking of a variety of interpretations within drum beats and variations within a given drum beat.

By their very nature constellations change in size and shape over a long period which is also apt in our description of our drumming constellations. In that, I mean that every exercise variation and every drum beat will hopefully over time grow, improve and so the drummer will advance in its application wherever or whenever the particular beat is used.

And like some constellations at one time where popular, others were dropped in place of the favored constellations, or in our terms we group the rhythms we prefer and put aside others that although served our improvement purposes and goals are not readily usable within our playing whether that decision is made based on personal preference or because of a particular style that was adopted by the drummer. This implies the creation of your own personal favorite beats and rhythms built over time.

Featured Drummer Recommendations

Vinnie Colaiuta

I never really listened to a lot of variation when it comes to Vinnie Colaiuta but I did listen to him a lot with artists such as Frank Zappa (Joes Garage Part 1, 2 & 3 - a must listen, but not for the faint of heart), Robben Ford and Joni Mitchel.

I was kinda obsessed with the few albums I did have of the artists I just mentioned.

I believe that I loved Joni Mitchel because of the weird, folkish, harmonic type tones the band created backed by Vinnie Caliutas somewhat offbeat fills and solo techniques. Joe's garage was something completely different than the Joni Mitchel music but the complexity of the feels Vinnie created using straight eight as well as shuffle type beats were outstanding and drew me in for many years.

Different again was Robben Fords bluesy rock style backed by Vinnies driving rock and shuffle type beats that could progress into an awesome drum fill at any point is what attracted my attention so much and again for a couple of years.

I highly recommend at least a listen to Robben Fords Talk to Your Daughters album where Vinnie plays some awesome driving rock and shuffle style beats. They will definitely serve as an awesome demonstration of Vinnie's skill level and the contents of books 1-4 of the Time Space & Drums Series.

Of course, there are literally thousands of rock, as well as jazz style feels available but the examples, I include in this and other featured drummer sections give you a good idea of the standards to aim for as I only include the very best recommendations possible regarding a particular style or feel demonstration. And Vinnie is one of the best when it comes to personal style.

When I listen to his drumming, I feel that he almost took the drumming techniques and styles taught by others and threw them all away and then came up with something so close yet so far away from what many other drummers do or even think of doing. His drum fills are just as incredible and although scientifically exacting his feel overpowers everything that he plays to make it literally out of this world.

I often have the feeling that when he starts a drum fill that it's just not going to fit into the timing of the music, but of course it does fit perfectly.

Although I said earlier that I had little experience when it comes to listening to Vinnie Colaiuta, and that was true, I still included him here as listening to his playing might help you to improve the way you play the rock style beats, we included in this book.

To some degree, this is a development set of lessons but in reality, it is simply a further development of the foundation on which you will later build your own styles and feels and how you personally interpret your basic playing techniques. Vinnie is a perfects example of this basic idea but of course, he advances it like I said, out of this world which is also fitting for the Time Space & Drums series.

I place building a solid foundation above all else throughout this series of books but that foundation is really a launch pad for you to launch your own personal style and way of doing things later. This, of course, all starts with how you like the drums to sound and what your experimentation uncovers regarding the basic foundational concepts as you develop your own foundation of drumming skills and abilities.

As suggested throughout the Modern Drumming Concepts book there are basic fundamentals to follow but never be afraid to add your own twist to things especially as you grow and your experience with the basic fundamentals and concepts solidifies and gets internalized by you. You are after all the real instrument of your drumming.

Conclusion

If you are reading this passage because you have completed this book then give yourself a pat on the back. There was a lot to cover. I was originally going to make two parts to this book. This was a challenge for me to write, so from a beginner's point of view, it must have been a really big challenge.

Now that you have completed the book I would recommend going back to the beginning and playing everything again with the RH Ride Cymbal and the left foot playing 1, 2, 3, and 4 on the LF HH as suggested earlier.

For future reference, you could also repeat everything playing the LF on the "off-beat" instead of on 1, 2, 3 and 4. However this isn't necessary at present, but do bear it in mind for the future.

It is now time for you to start developing the Jazz style beats covered in book 2. And I would recommend that you get down to it straight away while you are still buzzing from completing this book. Or you may be too exhausted so may need a break. Either way I wish you luck and will see you next time.

Remember Success Breeds Success. Keep Going and Have fun.

Stephen Hawkins

Closing Note:

The Time Space and Drums series is intended as a complete program from Part 1 to Part 12. It is strongly advised that you follow the program in order of the parts as they integrate and build on each other. The only thing I can now add is to practice each exercise until you have them all mastered. Mastery comes from paying attention to the most basic fundamentals already covered in each of the exercises within this book.

Once you have perfected each exercise you may like to try them left-handed but that may take time depending on your current skill level.

Free Audio Demonstrations

Please don't forget to visit the following URL to download audio demonstrations of every exercise in this book as soon as possible. You will then receive some additional tips and guidance through the included essence emails.

www.timespaceanddrums.com/tsd-3rt.html

What's Next

Thank you for choosing Time Space and Drums as one of your learning tools. I hope you enjoyed the process. You can explore more of the series in Constellations Volume Two, the fourth book in the series by searching for "**Jazz Drumming Development**" at your favorite bookstore.

Share Your Experience

If you have a moment, please review this Rock Drumming Development book at the store where you bought it. Help other drummers and tell them why you enjoyed the book or what could be improved. Thank you!

Thank you again dear reader and I hope we meet again between the pages of another book. Remember, You rock!

Other Books by The Author

Modern Drumming Concepts
Rock Drumming Foundation Series part. (Six in-depth Drum Lessons).
Jazz Drumming Foundation Series part. (Six in-depth Drum Lessons).
Rock Drumming Development Series part. (Six in-depth Drum Lessons).
Jazz Drumming Development Series part. (Six in-depth Drum Lessons).
Odd Time Drumming Foundation Series part. (Six in-depth Drum Lessons).
Music Minus Drummer Collection. (Six in-depth Drum Lessons).
Accents and Phrasing Series part. (Four in-depth Drum Lessons).
Basic Latin Drumming Foundation Series part. (Four in-depth Drum Lessons).
Developing Creativity Volume 1. (Four in-depth Drum Lessons).
Developing Creativity Volume 2. (Four in-depth Drum Lessons).
Developing Creativity Volume 3. (Five in-depth Drum Lessons).
Developing Creativity Volume 4. (Six in-depth Drum Lessons).

Printed in Great Britain
by Amazon